Within Reach

Within Reach

Poems by M.J. Iuppa

Cherry Grove Collections

Published by Cherry Grove Collections
P.O. Box 541106
Cincinnati, OH 45254-1106

ISBN: 9781934999875
LCCN: 2010923089

Poetry Editor: Kevin Walzer
Business Editor: Lori Jareo

Visit us on the web at www.cherry-grove.com

Acknowledgments:

Grateful thanks to the editors of the publications where these poems first appeared, sometimes in earlier versions:

Blueline, Buckle &, The Café Review, The Centrifugal Eye, The Coffee House (U.K.), The Comstock Review, Cyclamens & Swords, 5 A.M., Flint Hills Review, Fourth River, HazMat Review, The Iconoclast, Into the Teeth of the Wind, miller's pond,The Modern Review (Canada), Oak Bend Review, Old Red Kimono, The Paterson Literary Review, Pearl, Pebble Lake Review, Poetry Midwest, The Potomac Review, The Puckerbrush Review, Rosebud, Sea Stories, Tar River Poetry, Tar Wolf Review, and *Wordwrights*

"Mother's Dream" first appeared in *Voices in the Gallery: Writers on Art,* edited by Grant Holcomb, University of Rochester Press, 2001.

"Staying in Someone's Brownstone" first appeared in *Night Traveler,* Foothills Publishing, 2003.

"The Day Before They Declared War" *The Making of Peace: Poetry Broadside Series*, edited by Kelli Russell Agodon, April, 2006.

"Pond" collected in *From the Other World: Poems in Memory of James Wright,* edited by Bruce Hendricksen and Robert Johnson, Lost Hills Books, 2007.

"Thundercloud" *Le Mot Juste Anthology*, 2007.

"Groundwork" *Le Mot Juste Anthology*, 2008.

"round go merry" first published in *The Poets Guide to the Birds*, edited by Judith Kitchen and Ted Kooser, Anhinga Press, 2009.

"Bleach" collected in *Eating Her Wedding Dress: A Collection of Clothing Poems,* edited by Vasiliki Katsarou, Ruth O'Toole, and Ellen Foos, Ragged Sky Press, 2009.

Cover Art: *Magnolia II,* K. Iuppa © 1994.

I wish to thank several people whose advice, encouragement and friendship helped me to complete this collection: Peggy Shumaker, Sharon Bryan, Susan Ludvigson, Judith Kitchen, Stan Sanvel Rubin, and The Rainier Writers Workshop.

for Peter Tonery

Table of Contents

1

Artifacts..17
The Season of Mud...............................18
Single steps..19
Bleach...20
Button...21
The Crab Apple Tree...........................22
What the Chinese Call Earth's Nails....23
Barter..24
Overhead..25
Threshold...26

2

Translation..29
Thundercloud...30
Two Canoes...31
Full Moon...32
Another Side of Morning......................33
The Contest...34
Taking a slow drive to the market........35
The Usual..36
round go merry......................................37
The Daydream..38
Mother's Dream.....................................39
Aftertaste..40
End of Autumn.......................................41
One Blue Spruce.....................................42
The Orchard..43
Snow is falling—everywhere................44

3

The Day Before They Declared War.....47
Among the Missing...............................48
Star(e)..49
Groundwork..50
January Sun 51
Christening..52
Hyacinths..53
Fishing, still...54
Gone...55
Blind (Wo)man's Bluff...........................56
Outside, the world quivers 57
February..58
View from a Hilltop...............................59
Eclipse...60
Back Yard Feeder..................................61
I saw Quebec City rise up.....................62
The View..63
Staying in Someone's Brownstone.......64

4

In the Warm Yellow Kitchen on
    Aberdeen Street.................................67
Niagara...68
Tides...69
Plunge..70
Walking in the Neighborhood..............71
Flight 83: New York to Seattle..............72
Creation..73
The Log Stranded on the Beach
    Became Our Bench.............................74
Near the Open Window........................75
Below Sleep's Surface...........................76
Sun in Flowers above Water..................77
Pond..78

Explaining the flight of bats to someone
       who rarely flirts with danger..........79
The Weight of the World........................80
Oriental Bells and the Light
       of Mute Swan's Wings 81
The Nature of the Body.........................82
End of Summer: Rain............................83
By Any Means.......................................84
For Some Reason...................................85
Encore 86

1

Artifacts

From the worn treads of my shoes
clots of mud come loose
and fall onto the plank floor.

Fragrance of earth, remnants,
last straw of winter—
visible marks shrinking to questions.

I can't say why, but
pinch a piece to feel its powder
crumble between my fingertips.

Grit I brush onto my pants,
a gesture to keep whoever's missing
within reach.

The Season of Mud

Waking early, before the burble of birds percolates
into full song, before the lake sky awash in the belly

color of trout brightens to blue, I see everything
drying out. We may get a head start

at our slow age, turning over the gardens,
preparing the raised beds for this year's

casual crop of just what we need:
two to four kinds of every vegetable found

ripe and ready in seed catalogs.

It's those *must have* plump orange tomatoes
and creamy white eggplants that tempted us

when snow filled our windowsills,
and we could barely make our way out back—

Drifts cresting like ocean waves,
but that was weeks ago . . .

Now bundled packets in yesterday's mail,
and we've quit complaining.

A good sign, since we have so much work to do.

Single steps

I've awakened before the alarm, before the first bluing
of morning light. Farmhouse quiet. The wooden

floor, cold and weathered, moans beneath my hesitant
steps. The yellow dog raises her head in puzzlement:

                                    She snuffles a bit,
thumps her tail three times, then settles back to sleep . . .

In all this, nothing disturbs him, not sound, or movement
or clumsiness. I envy his ability to breathe deeply, evenly,

swimming beyond the depths of this world, without
concern of my leaving first . . .

Wide awake, I watch the silver remains of night
smolder to powdery ash. In the distance, the whole

landscape labors to come back in its old and approaching
shades of bluegreenbrown. Unfailingly, it pushes me

toward another threshold—sky, a stretch
of fields, open road.

Bleach

A speck. No bigger
than the head of a pin.

                  Bright.
I can see through it,
like a knot-hole.

Like a beacon, it shines
                  a distance
    on this shirt.

"Bleach," you say, touching
            the spot
            just above
            my heart.

Button

Today, I lost a navy blue enameled button off my shirt
and I worried . . .

No larger than a juju, this button, the perfect one,
 the knob of opening and closing . . .

Somewhere between picking up my sister at the airport
and the threshold of my dying brother's bedroom,
it was gone . . .

Slipped away like a shadow in April's twitching daylight.
I can't replace it. Not with a collar button's tightness, nor
with a last button's afterthought . . . I fidget.

My brother tells my sister that we've missed her . . .

He tells me I have four buttons left.

The Crab Apple Tree

This morning, after night's steady drizzle, the warm May air
is utterly still—and in that stillness in the back yard, the aging

crab apple's bright pink petals seduce our middling minds
to look up into the tree's crown and see ruby-throated

hummingbirds candling blossoms, sparks of light,
like birthday wishes caught in the frenzy of hands

clapping—and suddenly more bluster—blue jays
and cardinals toppling headlong into somersaults,

chasing each other limb to limb, scattering a spray of petals
that spin crazily onto the ground, leaving us a brief trail—

before we're doomed to another season's whispering
green shadows.

What the Chinese Call Earth's Nails

In defiance of boundaries,
trimmed yards, something fierce
erupts overnight—

       Fevered, like a rash,
like a thousand dazzling suns spinning
hypnotic sparks of light;
making us dreamy for an afternoon
with nothing to do—tempting us
to be found out of place—sprawled childlike
in the yard among dandelions, wild
yellow & blowzy white, deciding
which one to pick for a wish
or a necklace of wishes—

Such currency multiplies in
whirlwind where seeds sprout
sharp toothed roots
to anchor ground in places
distant and forgotten, refusing
to leave quietly, holding us, still.

Barter

Leaning against the wain wagon, leaning
    close enough to hear the hum drift—the bees
hot sparks above the ripe red haven peaches—

she takes her sweet time . . . It's hot
    and the farmer's son is simply setting out, waiting
on her gesture.

They oblige each other without adding their lives together,
    without stretching their differences in fuzzy talk,
weather, what not . . .

They are not the same moving in the shadows, passing
    the basket from hand to hand—they are not pretending—
not for one minute—taking that one hard look at one another.

Overhead,

      barn swallows float in slip-knot turns
above the gray cat slouching towards home . . .

                  In perpetual circles,
shadows cull the afternoon where two

swallows become six, unfolding
dusky air to blurred commotion.

                  The cat pauses
like glassy-eyed porcelain in its diminished

steps, pretending to be invisible
in this yard that revs with such shrill,

frantic cries that I'm uncertain
what will survive the moment.

Threshold

Before night fell, before heat and shadows
                      burned hard into birth's fever, it was too late:
In the open field, a cow lay unmoving—
                      the others wandered slowly away—

                                their fresh born lowed and mewed.

Our steady eyes roved the herd, hesitating
                        above her body's stillness.

We moved closer, drawn to witness
                  what had happened in a moment's cruel nature—

finding her—engorged pupil, foamy tongue,
                      twist of hoof and looped cord prolapsed—

lifeless among the erratic flight of meadow bees—this sight
                      measured against day's failing light.

2

Translation

What survives without leaving a trace?
The hall clock's second hand keeps proper rhythm,

the tic, tic leans back to trim the seconds
of good standing. You are here, they say, living

within a mind that lives within the body.
What was it? Your pupils narrow.

Again, the absence of divine touch;
The hellish swirl of contradictions.

Your offspring busy,
their hands touching everything.

How you hated to be picked on.
Crows at the window looking in.

Thundercloud
—Lake Ontario

A morning loaded with tension: electricity
of swallows cauterizing air—

                    The deceptively cool
lake, motionless, absorbing the hatching
shadow
of a thundercloud—
            bristling wind, bolt of searing light
               distills this steely defiance

to just so many raindrops.

Two Canoes

This evening, the lake's glassy surface
swallows the sky's silence. I see
two canoes listless in the water . . .

Over the mountains, shadows slide
into the recesses of hemlock and pine
and brood where the wind has lost

its language—

I stand with my arms loose at my sides
and notice one of the canoes drifting
away from its dreary station . . .

It floats detached—

a little awkward
in its turning away . . .

Full Moon

Awake in the middle of the night
when the air stands still and moist
and the moon's full light

floods the rolling acres of corn—dark
green leaves undulating in their slow
swell that mirrors water, but is suspect

in these sleepless hours when little
moves beneath the surface,
beneath the skin. Season of stupor,

relentless and narrow in its prospects,
offers carousing dreams that stagger
like those purple shadows pooling

on the soft shoulders of the empty road,
where wildness sprouts chicory's tufted
blues and buttercups that thrive in this

heat, and cicadas'
pixilated song
louder, all the night long.

Another Side of Morning

Outside
this little window, morning
floats on the scent of fresh
cut hay and heat that's lasted
through the barefoot night,
rippling over cornfields,
a shimmering green that undulates
and rolls, continually changing
in the crystal blue air where
a shock of blackbirds bursts
forth—scattering in all
directions, in the dark
rumble of the land cannon's
thunder, like the curtains' flutter—
thrown into a moment's confusion—
settles back into the shape of
folds, and like the fields are slightly
ruffled, showing another
side that's only seen when one
gets up to look.

The Contest

In slow-traveling weather,
the chemistry of clouds
festers silvery halos
that ring the mountains
in jeweled light.

> Below, lies a reckless sea
> of gray rocks—a labyrinth
> made worldly and ungodly
> in its passage.

Here, one stray voice burns feverishly
in the ear's cul-de-sac, making it
impossible to resist the contest
where one proves in breath and reach
the pitfalls of ascent.

Taking a slow drive to the market

for the usual bread, milk, and an easygoing
meal, where we'd sit on the porch with
our last two children and talk quietly about
what's holding us back from a day's satisfaction—

        And there, on the soft shoulder,
 I glimpse something furry and caramel brown,
and slow down to see its body wriggling—
front paws clawing forward, back legs frozen
and dragging, its leathery tail whipping around
and around, propelling itself toward a thick
mound of grass near the culvert.

        I nearly slip off the road, turning
around in a driveway where a man is busy sudsing
his dogcatcher truck, his chocolate lab jumping
and barking at the hose spraying ropes of water.

        They don't see me coming.
They aren't concerned about much.
        Oh, he says, turning away from me,
it's no big deal—that's just our crippled muskrat.

        I look back over my shoulder
to see the muskrat nestled nose down in the grasses—
chewing—eyes closed—ever-so-slowly—satisfied.

The Usual

after Edward Hopper's painting, *Seven A.M.*, 1948

Summer mornings burn bright, brighter and brighter
until blue shadows melt into the creases of this
whitewashed storefront, worn wooden steps,

old dirt road that leads to the edge of town
where an eye blink determines whether
you've been here for a minute, or your whole life . . .

A slight breeze ripples the air, raising a swirl of pink
dust. It hasn't rained in sixty days. Time is passing.
7 a.m. is the customary red bag brew of coffee—

8 a.m., the door unlocks—the oak counter smells like lemon oil.
The wide plank floors creak. The iron cash register pings
when the drawer springs open. What's special today?

Not shortcake. Haven't had shortcake in 54 years. Fresh
fruit in season. A stack of banana nut pancakes. Squeezed
juice. Buckwheat honey. Elderberry jelly. This is exclusive.

Oh sure, let's see . . . I'll have . . . the usual.

round go merry

flower sun, flower wild, some four watching bath bird foul.

pecker wood, finch gold, bird mocking mulberry row.

hold be, light flash, lookers on, vis-á-vis.

say nay, less need, dozen calls, as much so be.

bird humming light high, above suckle honey, less breath sigh.

The Daydream

Rain soaked, overgrown—
parsley, catnip, mint—

arching over the pond's short reach—a canopy
of green flecked with timid white blossoms

and bees drowsing in sweetness
that's offered like a quiet gesture—

Come here and sit still—
glimpse beneath this lush shade—

the water quivers like a daydream,
living inside, living outside,

the yearning of goldfish—
so many lips kissing the tranquil surface.

Mother's Dream

after Fairfield Porter's painting,
The Beginning of the Fields, 1973.

I know full well. I *am* getting away. No more fleeting moments.
Wishful thinking. My hands hold fast on the steering wheel's
backbone. The pressure of my open-toed shoe on the gas pedal
is exact. I am getting away in a white car on a summer road
that's the color of vinegar taffy. It stretches narrowly as it pulls
around a bend, offering me another direction.

*

The dome of sky is melon. The midday sun strikes, unblinking.
This is an annoying dead heat. A lone poplar stands sentinel.
My car's wheels turn on whispers. I don't care.

*

Away is clearly a race from here to there. It's my desire to set out
on my own, without intermission, until I see that what I've
dreamt at my desk, on my porch, in the back yard isn't a mirage.

*

Seeing the wind-swept fields erases tension. My hands relax
their grip. The tangle of grasses surround me. Over there, in the
half light, is my future.

Aftertaste

Picking berries without bruising them, my hand
slides blindly under dark ruffled leaves, feeling past
the dead to those hiding—I ignore my fingers' quick

pluck—the tumble of red fruit gleaming in a white bowl.
I'm doomed to spend the afternoon in this
appointed task when my head aches for another world . . .

Small red stains on my fingertips and the sun leather hot
on the back of my neck, I straighten up and look
back over my shoulder—

       There, Christmas trees are nearly grown
in a field full of milkweed and chicory—wheat
swollen in its whispering swirl of so much gold—
inertia, bearable . . .

            Without thinking,
I drop one plump berry on my tongue—its raspy
kiss melts, ever so slowly.

End of Autumn

Once again, tuning up the garden with black compost
and bags of neighbors' leaves, we work all afternoon

preparing raised beds to hold anonymous
spring bulbs, bought in bulk, lying

in a scatter on the barn's cement floor,
skins glowing silver in the approaching twilight.

These bulbs will mostly be forgotten.
Beyond our windows, beneath

snow's insulation, they'll sleep one season
into the next, until the earth warms

and they quicken
to blossom, bright and fragrant, thrilling

in their given names—*tulips, hyacinths,
daffodils*—and we'll

be shocked by their vivid
presence, loving briefly.

One Blue Spruce

At the solstice, in a woods we planted
years ago, I heard the red tailed hawk's cry
against the peerless morning sky—

                  And I could barely speak,
intoxicated by the smells of cold and evergreen,
sounds of past Christmases, where the dead remembered
on that walk pinched our cheeks red—our blood heated
to the task of picking the perfect tree . . .

Was this ritual for them or us? Were we any closer
to having our own lives, or is this still their bidding?

I counted eleven rings, from the pith to the edge
of bark, unfolding like a prayer—amber sap yielding
quiet tears that hardened into our living here.

The Orchard

Winter light, tincture of gray,
watery shadows cling
to the apple trees.

I stand here wide awake
at the threshold
of the longest night, listening

to one cardinal's chipped
notes float dusky green
in this chilly overcast,

remembering the past
in the corridor of miniature trees—
those pressing shadows—

the eerie height
of my older sisters bending
to shush me away

from discovering the fragrant
windfall underfoot—
pungent apples gone caramel,

taut skins ready to explode
at the mere touch of hand or hoof
or black tongue . . .

Snow is falling—everywhere

In the field, beneath the lone oak,
two horses stand transfixed—heads

bowed, foreheads pressing against
each other, drawing a plume of

breath that is one breath, curling
in the blueness of afternoon—

the soft, blurred outline of tree
and horses is a glimpse of a world

banking silence as its prayer
against the gathering

storm

3

The Day Before They Declared War

In a small restaurant called Aladdin's,
I sat alone at a table between
corner windows and looked down on
the canal's frozen water basking in direct
sunlight—its slow melt
trickled into thin silver streaks that
puddled at the foot of
a rock where a hundred webbed
footprints walked around and
around and around . . .

                    Are you ready? he asked,
                    Do you know what you want?

Among the Missing

Sitting in winter's dark, listening
to the wind chafing
beneath old clapboards,
and the thunder of the town's plow
scouring its way down the road's
ribbon of darkness

like a battleship navigating
its way west,
in spite of snow,
in spite of its dim lantern light
until it disappears completely—

And the open fields stand
unmarked, glistening
under the swell of the moon
riding the wake of navy
blue clouds, leaving
a trail of shadows
that settles in the corners
of an old farmhouse.

Star(e)

The boy is looking hard at the word **STAR** printed
in block letters on the yellow flash card. He is standing
on one foot, poised like a heron fishing. Dark hair
falling into his eyes, he squints. The teacher is barely
breathing, waiting on his one word. He says, "Stare."
And I am, staring at them; then at a loose note in my hand
that's rumpled with a message scrawled in black ink,
Don't worry. "Don't worry," she says, "Try again."
I look up. He says, "Star."

Groundwork

The fence that wasn't a barrier, that didn't hold
anything back or up, but was the grid over the scene of

smoke rising, smoldering from September
to December, as the slow green trucks crawled

back, and forth, churning up gray dust, heaving
lumps of cement, twisted iron beams, crushed

glass, bits of paper floating in the swirl
of tires rumbling past us, who stood on iron milk crates,

straining to see into the pit, staring into the silence of
the gathering crowd, into the rainless faces,

the on-going thoughts, what couldn't be imagined
or said out loud, not now, not in that hour, or the next—

faces still searched the blue patch of sky, that gaping
space above it all, and right before us, the fence

that held a single sunflower.

January Sun

Ghosts of ice
glisten on the bones

of sunflowers,
thistles, and burdock—

all leaning
forward

against
the worn

fence. Nothing
moves—not chimney

smoke from last night's
banked fire, nor the tongue

of the church bell—
not even black birds

sitting plumped
in the ancient maple's crown.

This cold unflinching—
the branches' sudden quiver.

Christening

In the kitchen's yellow light, I iron
the christening gown for the first time, praying
not to scorch its antique linen and ribbons
that have endured another bleaching . . .

        I close my eyes,
imagining my mother's weathered hand pressing
this dress into something petal soft and creamy
as a gardenia. . . .

The shush of steam startles me
to see my hand like hers on the iron, turning deftly
along the hem, heading toward the capped sleeve's
crimped edge . . .

And I am relieved when it is done.
       This is the miracle
         no one speaks of.

Hyacinths

Forgotten on the sill in the kitchen's cool spot,

the hyacinths planted
        in a white ceramic bowl
                hatch slowly—

Five green beaks
        with sharp egg teeth
                crack the crowns
                    of their purple bulbs
and stretch their necks long, and longer,
           housing the pith and breath
                  that feeds the spiked

fragrance of their brash sapphire heads—utterly Mozart.

Fishing, still

like apostles, they sit on buckets,
side by side, for hours, floating
on the waxy slab of ice
that shudders under the rub
of their weight, sinking in slush
that pools beneath their feet

And they wait, baiting each other
with swigs of ale, thumbing their lines
that drift by degrees, casual in the current

that swells and dips below the surface
of that dilating blue black eye

Gone

Snow falling—feathery & dizzy—glitter
thrown in a gesture of abandon . . .

At this time of year, in winter's pivoting
motion of thaw & freeze, dark-eyed juncos
frequent the backyard feeder. They hop &
twitter like chipping sparrows in the snag of
bare branches, working the tension of wire
to trip a spray of seeds.

Below, constellations of millet & milo & cracked
corn, the shape of survival. What drops upon
this threshold moves sideways, head cocked &
ready.

Under the porch's crouch, the shadow of
the cat . . .

Blind (Wo)man's Bluff

Snow falling all morning
in the wind, the windowpane

fern crystals bent in
a waver of weather, visible

chill testing the view—
isolated

thoughts of never
going back

on hard words—
a confused

buzz hangs in her ears—
She *must*

move—eyes
closed—arms outstretched.

Outside, the world quivers in the winter wind

its frosty tones crackle
through the maples' silvered
branches—tipping the small bells'
tongues to summon attention—

          Intensely now
and clear in a pocket of cold air
the *link, link, link*
calibrated in its petition—
its mad insinuation
that you've grown staid
in your ways—unable
to stir the dream of that fragrant
orchard where contentment
sidles with shadows &
the world holds its breath
beyond your sense of breathing—

          You face
those raw recriminations
at the window's hour—
old anxieties bone white—
Nothing you say now is
without a price.

February snow blows slant, scuffing
                    across these gouged fields, pressing

its slick piracy into the furrows'
          dark race, fixing blued waters to marble veins that trace
                    like waves caught in undercurrent,
                                        like thoughts left unanswered

                    What do we want
when we part the curtains to stare out the window?

View from a Hilltop

Midmorning. The wind ruffling through the cottonwoods sounds like rain. Church bells toll the hour of eleven, yet haze still lingers on the distant fields of green and gold. The earth is damp under my feet. An ant, the color of honey, sidles up a sturdy blade of grass, hesitates. The edge of its world as vast as mine.

Eclipse

I saw an oily smudge of a man
bent over his shopping cart

He knew I was walking towards him
He knew I was alone

I slowed down a bit, uncertain
of what he would do

I listened to the scuffle of my feet

My body's hurried angle overshadowing
his being there

Back Yard Feeder

One by one, in bright daylight, nuthatches
    arrive at the back yard feeder, chipping away
in their discriminating taste—quick-picking milo

and white millet, spitting back sunflower seeds
    that stipple the fresh snow where juncos and sparrows
hop, gorging themselves on what they love best.

They too take their turns, swinging on the feeder, spilling
    the excess for the others—chickadees, finches, cardinals—
busyness—flitting in and out of the crab apple tree, waiting

and not waiting for their ride on this carousel
    that stops abruptly in the flash of wings spiraling
through the wiry branches, spraying wisps of snow in the swirl

of flight to everywhere but here. The yard stands empty—
    The sharp-shinned hawk settles onto a high branch, unruffled—
The feeder quivering slightly.

I saw Quebec City rise up

in its armor,
its hills glistening, silver
and gold, trails

of smoke
streaking against winter's
indigo sky . . .

       And far below,
at the foot of the city,
the St. Lawrence's sinewy
tension, its icy hold

tendered sorrow's cargo
in the brilliance of salt
water, and somewhere deep
beneath that ceiling of ice, ancient
sturgeon suspended
in dim recesses, stony gaze
& lock jawed—

ponderous & stiff—
indifferent, yet
watchful . . .

The View

Never sat like this before, in a quiet window seat,
34 floors above Manhattan, looking North

on Central Park, on silhouettes of skyscrapers glowing
silver in December's smoldering light, and realized

that this city has survived on architecture's oldest lines,
as language is the conversation of a hundred native cities

spoken street to street, so is the steel, brick, and mortar—
something completely human—an arterial map rooted

in this island's bedrock, an undercurrent of life transfixed in
the steady rush of traffic that doesn't yield to silence

but rises up in decibels and muscle
to pass through every noon's hour.

Staying in Someone's Brownstone

Not for long—becomes longing for comfort,
longing, where loneliness makes sure
of its routine, and nothing familiar, not table
or chair or green plants, graces
work with a sense of place, supper
with family, those bustling hours . . .

Something said about modern elegance
when you are the oldest object in the kitchen:
You back off chopping celery, carrot, onions
to push away errant strands of graying hair,
and stare at small red potatoes boiling in the black
pot; ground meat simmering in the skillet . . .
Steam hits you in the face and you think—
Is this a joke? —

Eating alone in a city that has occasional friends
who expect more than shepherd's pie & small talk,
you sit in the candlelight; listen hard for the car's
security beep & door slam—the exhaust of getting away—
knowing that you've paid dearly to be here on your own,
lifting a stranger's silver spoon to your mouth.

4

In the Warm Yellow Kitchen on Aberdeen Street

I sat in a corner, cross-legged on a wooden chair,
leaning on the white enamel table pushed

against an inside wall; and above, an open shelf
displayed blue willow plates and a small carved

knickknack of three monkeys, *see no evil,*
hear no evil, speak no evil, and I listened to family

conversations, nearly unnoticed, and drank milk with
a double dose of coffee and swore to my aunt that

I wouldn't tell, because I knew that it would be
the end if I did, and I didn't want time to end there,

in that kitchen, with Sunday chicken roasting in the oven
and the glossy black & white checkered linoleum floor

daring me to hop on one foot over two squares and back
to my seat where I felt the rhythm of everything not left out.

Niagara

I.

Under daylight's white glare, the rapids'
hard boil
is blue thunder, spelling
its quarrel with a world
that listens
obliquely.

II.

Shadows flirt
like heartbeats, like faint blue whispers
teasing us to stand at the doorway,
witness the horizon blossoming orange.

The river below,
flat and arrested, without pulse
is sliced open
by a thumbnail moon.

Everything left unsaid
is, at last, understood.

Tides

A sweep of rain turns city streets oily and slick.
Sycamores lining close to the curb undress slowly
in the shadows of brownstones.

                          She is invisible, standing
in the dark, at the third floor bedroom window, watching
the street's decision match her own.

                          In a room across the way,
an unseen hand taps the sensor switch, plucking
seconds—breathless strands—electricity.

Moisture blooms on glass:
Below, footsteps to Third Avenue quicken—
Someone's leaving, just before morning.

Plunge

At the cocktail party, you were there, swimming
in the company of suits and simple black dresses.

Confident, skirting the ripple of laughter, ducking
under the thin veil of smoke and pungent

bite of perfume.
                          You floated on the edge of
conversations—mouths moving in an undercurrent

of words sliding beneath the rushes where
surface sounds emerged for one distinct moment:

the searing pop of ice cubes in sweaty glasses—
gold bracelets *shushing* in the slight gesture

of the well-meaning song that gave you
your opportunity to be seen—And so,

you broke the surface of that inner circle neatly—
drifting a bit, until an arm circled your waist

and pulled you closer.

Walking in the Neighborhood

High in the treetops, against the flat blue sky, cicadas
announce their pesky presence in a steamy shimmer

that's white hot as the light that blanches our faces—
we look cautiously around the playground . . .

                    Only leaves flicker *home free*,
and low-riding cars bounce in raps' back beat thumps

while three-on-a-bike spin a slow zigzag across Atlantic's
blacktop, catching the swell of garlic smothered

in oil & tossed with three colored tortellini
that taste the same as one color yellow

served al dente to those who can decipher a stomach
growl in traffic's rumble

past Edibles & beyond
the Forum and street signs:

No standing here to corner.
                    No motorcycles on the sidewalk.

No white chalk drawings or yellow police tape.
                  Only starfish on window ledges,

giant wooden coffee cups, iridescent
butterfly chairs, *Celebrity*

strewn upon *In Style* on glass top tables—
Our wish for a difference every day.

Flight 83: New York to Seattle

Confined to the window seat over the wing,
I'm startled by the spectacle of clouds, ripe
with lightning, and imagine rain falling
straight, like thin needles
on the hemmed farmland
below—
       We're skimming above
this summer storm, unfettered
by its phosphorus explosions—
Our flight outdistancing
earth's turmoil—

The young woman
next to me
sleeps so soundly.

Creation

after *"The Architect's Brother,"*
a photograph by Robert ParkeHarrison

The architect's brother,
living in a honeycomb of thought,
exists in a single cell, cold and still;

eyes shut, forehead pressed
to that silence quickening—
wing beats, wasp breath—

thin strands of spittle spun
to seal his fate—He is drone,
a photographer, nearly forty, blind
in the eye of his making.
Haunted that he will never
capture radiance—That life,
springing from a fistful of dirt.

The Log Stranded on the Beach
Became Our Bench

for Kay and Margie, at Point Defiance

We sat there, middle-aged, side
by side, our bare feet coated with gritty

bits of stone and talked about how we left
our settled lives without looking at each other.

No, we looked straight ahead—
over the slow-moving water, ignoring

the crowd sounds punctuated
by comings and goings of small boys dragging

long ropes of kelp, and that yellow dog
barking, *stop, stop* as the canoe's bow lifted

onto shore. We sat there motionless, staring
at the quivering gray water, the canoe, the dog;

imagining the narrow space one has
to make in that sudden leap

of faith, watching the dog's flight—
her landing inches from the water.

Near the Open Window

Alone, in a hot dormitory cell, I slept on my back,
on top of two flat sheets that made a narrow bed;

imagining I was lying in a wooden boat, floating
into a dream I wanted while listening to the sprinklers'

gush and those red footed pigeons' coo,
plump and sober, near the open window . . .

                              In fitful turns, I woke
every half hour, skirting the outline I made for myself—

dumbfounded by the wad of sheets rising into a mound
under the small of my back—its incursive spell left me

stranded, teetering on the brink of night's undoing until
my two dumb feet found the slippery tile, and I stood

there in morning's twilight, wondering if a drink of cold
water would be enough before the day began bright

and full of detours that forced me to look beyond
my beguilement, beyond my sleeplessness, beyond

the open window's speech that petitioned me nightly
to come closer—no, no, closer.

Below Sleep's Surface

This is limbo, this sound of
      breath and whale song, echoing
            against the ocean floor, lungs filling

A child calling in the dream, the corridor
      of light, sea foam green and murmuring
            seaweed—like long dark hair floati

freely above me—two feet below
         the surface of sleep, heart twisted raw
          by the cries of the child locked out,

whose eyes open and close on the dreams of the forgotten,
    like this, like this, like this, waiting
       in limbo, dreaming,

the silence of things, slipping,
      slipping, out of my extended
      hands, out of reach.

Sun in Flowers above Water

In fate's window, memory clouds.
Her private conversation fogs the glass.
The compass points fail in this odyssey,
a mental murder, the stain of strawberries
on fingertips.
        "Where did this come from?"
She looks at her raw hands.
        "What have I done?"

Outside: sun in flowers above water.

Pond

In day's broad light, in heat, without threat of more rain,
my husband works alone, clearing
weeds and rocks near the split rail fence.

He digs a neatly carved pit and calls it Pond,
filling its kidney shape with water and cattails,
and goldfish won at the firemen's fair.

Under the wide shade of a white umbrella,
he snakes a garden hose up under a terrace of rocks,
turning the water's spray to perpetual music.

I like to look into this pond with my weariness.
I like to watch the clouds in its quiet face.
I like to see the flash of bright

orange, streaking
out of the shadows
just beyond my sight.

Explaining the flight of bats to someone who rarely flirts with danger

Summer of heat and lightning but no rain, only
fireflies blinking on and off in evergreen shadows

that loom over the narrow canal's murky water where
our idle boat passes into twilight, carrying the weight

of our misgivings.
                              We are quiet—our thoughts

folded inward—like bats, waiting
for the shimmering hour to fly —like rain

caught in wind—weightless bodies,
vanishing in the blink of an eye.

The Weight of the World

In one crevice of all the chinks and clefts on this barren dome,
windblown dirt lined a pocket of darkness where
a pine no bigger than a toe found its hold
and grew ancient.

        There, boughs trained to the wind's rage
became resilient in the crouch of a sentinel—forever watchful,
faithful as if the shadow of the pine were a woman's silhouette, lying
on her back, looking up through the boughs to that space
that defies gravity.

Oriental Bells and the Light
of Mute Swan's Wings

How brave, the divine idol and idle thought met last night.

Obscure light wasn't nectar, rather vulgar
undoing, leaving one on one's side—a finished piano—

hoarse strings sprung:

> *Amplify and nod,*
> *Amplify and nod*

Those giant wings flourished in this myth's undertow.

The Nature of the Body

While in the garden in late August,
intoxicated by the perfume of leaf
and fruit, I find myself yearning . . .

             My body collapsed
into its smaller self—fingers cramped
to pluck peppers with a clean pinch—
desire, the nature of the body,
and the pepper in my hand
 no longer anonymous and green . . .

Tracing its smooth line, I see
the silhouette of supple flesh
turn tenderly into buttocks
and shoulders, revealing
what I truly want—
two heads tipped in a deep kiss.

End of Summer: Rain

Waking to the sound of *thunk, thunk*—
                    oversized drops, landing
                              squarely
                                in the blue tin cup left
                on the glass table, I hear

                          a lone car speeding by,
                    casting a spray
                        of water caught in its wheels—

        I listen closely, thinking—
                    if I don't see you, I'll see you soon.

By Any Means

In a field the farmer left fallow for two seasons,
abundance: a meadow of wild carrot

whispering Queen Anne's desire to bear a child.
Her thoughts, while tatting by an open window,

revealed in her handiwork those white lace flowers
spin under July's sun like parasols, shielding

the tenderness of timothy and blues of chicory
growing there, unexpectedly—
                              a field of promise,
full of insects' polished songs, the flight

of damselflies glittering in sunlight, resting
briefly on the flowers' frills; gracing

each center's three drops of blood—
this was Queen Anne's will

to create out of nothing—
this idle field, so full of life's sympathies.

For Some Reason

Deep within the thicket, small towers of
pastel-colored bee boxes lean precariously

on cleared ground, shivering
under the sudden scuffle of leaves & bits of light

exploding in the flight of goldfinches worrying
their comings & goings, their cautionary tales

spelled in a summer afternoon above bee boxes
swaying with the sound of bees

perfectly clover, making
every cell golden

Encore

Awakening in a rumpled hour, rising
like Lazarus to the automatic
drip of coffee, sucking its breath—alive

in heartbeats that trip start a body dragging
like a load of dirt, like the chugging
thump of the iron furnace igniting . . .

Will it catch on one more time;
send a blast of dry heat up through the registers
to warm the tick in these old wooden floors?

This roaming the farmhouse before God's hour
of light merely skims the surface of things
left undone—O Lazarus, look how what you

thought you left behind haunts you now—
everything brimming with expectations—
hall clock clapping its hands.

M.J.Iuppa lives on a small farm near the shores of Lake Ontario. She has four chapbooks and one full-length poetry collection, *Night Traveler* (Foothills Publishing, 2003). In 1996, she was the recipient of the Writing In Rochester Award, honoring a teacher of writing for adult students who has impacted the creation and appreciation of literature in Rochester; and, at St. John Fisher College, she has received the Part-Time Faculty Award for Teaching Excellence, May 2000; The Father Dorsey Award, 2000-2001 and 2002-2003, and a Certification of Recognition from The Monroe County Legislature, April 2003. Currently, she is Writer-in Residence and Director of the Arts Minor program at St. John Fisher College, Rochester, New York.

CPSIA information can be obtained at www.ICGtesting.com
Printed in the USA
LVOW041543211211

260537LV00004B/1/P